HOW TO MAKE SERIOUS MONEY WITH BINARY OPTIONS

THINGS YOU NEED TO KNOW BEFORE YOU
START TRADING BINARY OPTIONS

TODD WILLIAMS

INTRODUCTION

The purpose of this book is to show you how to make money trading Binary Options. Binary Options are a popular investment instrument for trading stocks, commodities and currencies. Trading Binaries is very simple and straightforward; all you need to do is decide which of the two directions the asset will move, up or down. The great new is that binary options have quite a high profit potential.

Binary options allow even beginners the opportunity to succeed with financial trading. Actually people that have minimum financial track record can easily make money by learning how to trade options online.

This book features the in and outs of binary options as well as strategies needed to achieve success in trading binaries - potentially earning a lot of money.

WHAT IS BINARY TRADING?

Binary trading option, also called digital option, all-or-nothing-option, or fixed return option, is a type of option where one has only two means of payoff; you can either take a fixed amount of the asset or nothing at all. The trade will either rise or fall, or in binary trading language "call" or "put". For starters, there are two types of binary trading options available – cash-or-nothing and asset-or-nothing. However, there are four other options regularly traded in the market, these are double-one-touch/double two-touch, asset-or-nothing, no-touch and one-touch. Binary trading option is a type of option that follows European style options, meaning they worked only on their expiration date not before or after.

Binary trade option is one example of exotic option. It is a trading option that delivers unique characteristics making it complex and unmanageable. In terms of functionality, binary trade options appear to be simple to use and interpret. One thing to remember is that compared to traditional trading where the payout increases along with the stock value, in binary trading, a fixed amount is identified and that will be the only payout through and through.

Binary training method also provides instant results since it is conducted on a web-based environment. You can do it within your own home using a regular desktop computer or laptop. This trading option is simple and straightforward and learning how to trade is easy.

HOW DOES IT WORK?

When trading binary options, you need to specify a fixed payout that will be picked up by the traders when certain conditions are met. Just like in sports betting, you can easily determine if it is a "win" or a "loss". In the case of binary choices, the price will increase or decrease, based on what type of option was chosen. Below are some examples of binary trade options, with a brief explanation of how they are done and how much are their payouts.

Cash or nothing option

The cash or nothing option is the most common, if not the most traded binary options. Most traders, and those who are just about to start, use this option. In cash-or-nothing trading option, an exercise price or the asset price is given. This is the value of the asset when trading starts that day. You need to choose whether, at the end of the trading day the asset price will finish higher or lower than the initial price. In other words you need to predict whether the price will rise or fall by the end of the trading day. A correct prediction means you can earn the money allotted for the asset. Although the profits depend on the agreed price, this could usually range from 170%-190% of your original premium. If in case one miscalculates, and assumed wrong, or the price stayed the same, you can still find some sort of a refund. There are some trading companies that offer a 10-15% refund, but only for out of money trades. This option is the easiest to use, which is why it is considered the most profitable.

Asset or nothing Option

The asset-or-nothing option follows roughly the same principles as the cash-or-nothing option; the only difference is that there is no payoff unless the price of the underlying asset increased. This means that there is no option for "put" or a fall in an asset or nothing option. If the asset's value increased, one will receive the amount that corresponds to the new price of the asset. So even though you need to wager an amount, the earnings will be based on the actual price and not your bet.

OTHER TYPES **of Binary Option Trades**

Touch Options

No-touch option

The no-touch option is the exact opposite of one touch option. In this option, the trader needs to determine what amount his chosen asset will not reach on the date that he will determine. This is considered the riskiest among the binary options because one needs to anticipate what will happen to the market over a certain period of time. Profit becomes larger as the time frame becomes longer although the risk remains higher as time progresses.

One touch option

Another type of binary trade option is the "one-touch" option. Unlike when doing the cash or nothing option or the asset or nothing option, in the "one-touch" option one needs to forecast if the monetary value of an asset will reach an identified price before the expiry time. With this option one needs to identify the barrier or the price that needs to be reached, when it will be reached and how much will the payout be. That in mind, a correct prediction will give one a full payout while a wrong choice will lose one the full premium set initially. This type of option can make the most money possible – an increase of around 250-400% of the original amount.

Double no-touch option / Double one-touch option

Following the idea of one touch option, in a double touch option one needs to determine a value that the asset will touch during the course of a time frame the trader selected as well. The only difference is that in a double one-touch option, one needs to determine two values that he thinks the asset will reach before the maturity date. If the asset is able to reach one of the two predetermined values, he will receive the full payout; failure will mean loss of all premiums.

The double no-touch option on the other hand follows the concept of no-touch option. This time, however, two points are identified as unreachable. One will only get the payout when the time lapses and none of the points are reached.

Target Bet Option

Target binary option operates on the concept of predicting if the market will end in a positive range or a negative range.

Positive targets. A positive target implies that one speculates that an asset will end up within a positive range.

Negative target A negative target implies that one speculates that an asset will end up within a negative range

Ladder Bet Option

This is a type of binary trading option where the trader is given a price range arranged in equal intervals – just like staircases or ladders. Here, one needs to identify several price levels as well as several periods. A trader earns when the assets he chose have, "climbed" the ladder's steps at certain times he also set.

TUNNEL BET OPTION

In this option, a trader buys a contract. This contract states a price range. A trader either chose to believe that the asset's value will stay in that range or breaks through and passes the same range. Tunnel bet option is also known as In/Out option.

There are two variants of the in/out option. One is stays between/ goes outside. The other is ends between/ends outside. In a stays between/ goes outside variation, "stay between" means that price has to stay within the barrier set and should not touch the barriers while a "goes outside" as the name implies, require the value to touch the barriers before the trade expires in order to end in a profit. The ends between/ends outside variation on the other hand requires that the values of an asset be within the barrier or strictly be outside the top or the bottom barrier on trade expiration.

WHAT YOU NEED TO KNOW BEFORE TRADING BINARY OPTIONS

1. **Know your terms**

Before jumping into the proverbial river called binary trading, you must familiarize yourself first with the terms used in this trading platform. Besides learning about the kinds of binary trades (see chapter 1) you must also know how to use the language that professional traders use so you actually have an idea of what's going on.

At the money. This is the term used by binary traders use to describe breaking even. This happens when the value of the asset ended up the same as when it opened. When this happens the money is returned to the trader in full.

Call Option. A call option implies that the trader believes that the asset he chose will increase upon the specified time. The increase can be as small as a tenth of a cent, as long as the value increases the call is honored. If called correctly, then you will make a profit. And if you guessed wrong, then you lose all of the money that you wagered.

Expiry date. This refers to the time and date that the trader sets for when the binary option will expire. When this time comes, the price is examined to determine if one is "in the money" or "out the money". The expiry date can be as short as 15 minutes, or it can take as long as a week, maybe even longer, depending on your choice. The longer the time allotted, the higher the premium earned, but the risks will be higher as well.

In the money. Winning the trade is referred to as being "in the money". If a trader predicted that the value will increase, and it did, or if he predicted a decrease, and it happened, then he wins. This is considered a successful trade; hence it is "in the money".

Out the money. This is the opposite of "in the money". A wrong prediction of the rise or fall of an asset's value will mean that one is "out the money".

Pips. Pips refer to a unit of measurement. This is the measurement that tracks the increase or decrease of the value of the assets.

Put option. This is the exact opposite of the call option. In this case, the trader predicts that the value of the asset in question will decrease before the time is reached. Just like in a call option, an increase of a tenth of a cent means a profit for the trader.

Strike price. Strike price refers to the price point where the outcome of binary trade is decided. This is identified by the trader himself.

Touch option. In touch point, any trader just needs to decide if the asset's value will reach a specific mark, either below or above the opening price by the end of time. If the asset touches that point by the end of trade additional premium will be given to the trader.

1. **Know the trend**

After familiarizing yourself with the trading terms, you should also familiarize yourself with the financial market. One's success in predicting a "call" or a "put" is based on how one interprets the movement of the trade, and not relying on mere chance. Keep in mind that events, news, and controversies can affect assets and their values. These issues can affect the market trend. Read financial news, watch financial shows and listens to trade advice. One should focus on those that determine the possible trading commodities. Not being prepared means a 50% chance of losing. A return rate of below 100% is an indicator that one can lose money in the long run.

1. **How much money is needed?**

MOST PEOPLE WOULD AGREE that one needs to hold at least $1000 as trading capital, or $3000 if one wants to hold a really good stab at it.

1. **Know what options to Buy**

PART OF PREPARATION is knowing what to trade. Do not just go out to the market and take everything you want and add it to your portfolio. Familiarity with an asset can prove to be an advantage to the trader. Start with the popular and stable stocks. Just like in traditional trading, focusing on blue chips turned out to be beneficial to everyone. A great deal of information about these assets is readily available for traders, and you need to make use of as many resources as you can to increase your chances of success.

1. **Know your Tools**

MANY TRADING COMPANIES assist their customers by providing them with tools to do their own research and analysis. Make sure to take advantage of such opportunities. One should learn how to read a graph or a chart of a certain asset. These can give one an idea of a trend of an asset. Most brokers have their own tools they use. Make sure to check out what can give the most accurate result.

THERE ARE **several charts you could look at. Some are as follows:**

- BAR CHARTS – these includes all of the basic and standard trading information one needs to know. It indicates the opening price, closing price, the highs and the lows of an asset.

- **Candlestick chart**– same as a bar chart, candlesticks show the standard trading information such as high, low, open and close price of a stock. It is color coded to show whether the stock ended below the open price or above it.

- LINE CHART- THE LINE chart only provides the close price of an asset on a day-to-day basis. This could be helpful in assessing whether the price will increase or decrease the following day.

6. **Know the Signals**

Binary option signals help traders identify opportunities for profit before they actually happen. Companies that provide such service makes sure that their customers can get all the information they need regarding an asset, like what to buy, when to buy, and how much to buy are provided. These companies also make sure that their clients are updated through any means possible. They get in touch with their clients through, but not limited to SMS, phone calls, Skype and such.

There are three types of Binary option signals providers in the market today.

1. Automatic Trade software provider – This is the newest option provided for traders. This option uses software that could communicate with the trading platform. This way, trades could be triggered automatically.
2. Partial-Manual-Trade Providers – In this category, binary option signals provides trade alerts that are not clear-cut. They are just mere heads-up as to what will happen in the trade market. The decision on trading is still left with the trader
3. Full-Manual Trade Providers – this leaves the

entire decision up to the trader. The company will provide the price – for buying and selling – as well as when to buy or to sell. The provider sends the information to the trader through different means of communication possible, and then waits for the decision of their client trader. The only problem is if delivery of the signals comes across delays, the implementation of the trade will also be delayed. In addition to this, there is an issue about the accuracy of the signals and win-rates for the trade.

7. **Learn how to manage risk**

Unlike stock or foreign exchange trading where one can cut his loss when necessary, the binary trade option it is all-or-nothing. The rule of thumb when it comes to binary trading is that you should expose only 5% or less of your capital. Do not just shove everything out in the market, then hope and pray it works to your advantage.

3

THE ADVANTAGES & DISADVANTAGES OF BINARY TRADING

ADVANTAGES

Trade anywhere, anytime

Binary trading option makes use of an online trading platform that is accessible via desktop, laptop and even mobile phones. This gives traders convenient access and real time updates on his or her stocks. Even when traveling, you can easily check up on your trading options and make decisions on the fly. Assets included in binary trading are internationally traded. This means that trading through this option is a 24/7 affair.

ANY MARKET CONDITION **is trade able.**

Traditional trading platforms require an increase in stock before you can make a profit. When the market is experiencing a downfall, then your money will get put on hold. You need to wait until the market is up again before you can withdraw your earnings. And, if worst comes to worst, the value of your stocks won't rise again, and you just have to cut your losses and try again.

In binary trading, you can make money not just when the prices are on the rise, you can also earn even when the prices are falling. These opportunities equal greater profit earning potentials.

MINIMAL INVESTMENT

With binary trading most brokers allow their clients to trade with as little as $1 in their account. You can start with a small amount; remember to only trade using money that you can afford to lose.

EASY AND SIMPLE Trading via Binary option is as easy as 1, 2, 3:

1. Select your asset and the expiry date.
2. Choose your position; either call (increase) or put (decrease).
3. And then choose the amount you want to wager

Once done all you need to do is sit back and wait for the result.

A WIDE ARRAY **of Choices**

Binary trade option offers a wide range of locally and internationally traded; you only need to choose the ones that appeal to you. But do make sure that you check your options carefully.

. . .

Less Risk

Since only a minimal amount of money is required, you will only be risking as much as you can afford. When you choose an option, there will always be a potential for gain, and for loss as well. Keeping this is in mind will allow you to calculate the risks and figure out an amount that you are comfortable betting with.

HIGH REWARDS **and Fast Returns**

Traders can set their own time frame. The time frame can range from 15 minutes or up to a week. Within this period one can already see the returns of their premiums. Return rates, on average, ranges between 70 to 88%. Continuous return rates like this can make a substantial if not high return of investment for any trader.

DISADVANTAGES

No Time for Practice

Unlike traditional trading platforms where you can practice before the actual trading, in binary trading no simulated trading support is given by brokers to their traders. There may be companies that offer demo accounts, but they are very few and far in between. Traders enter the market without any practice. You basically learn as you go.

No Trading Tools

Charts and tools are not readily available for a binary options trader; you have to put out a request for them. Technical analysis is also not available for binary trading. Traders are kept virtually in the dark when using this type of trading platform.

Tools, charts and technical analyses are important tools of any trader. This can help predict a trend, when to stop or when to continue. Tools are particularly useful when one uses the "touch options" – one-touch, double one-touch, double no-touch, or no-touch. Chart analysis, technical analysis and trending lines can help predict what values the asset can reach or what values it will not reach over a period of time.

STUDYING **Financial Assets and Markets on your own is hard work.**

Since no studies, charts and analysis are available for any one's perusal, studying for this type of trade requires working from scratch. Studying is very important if one wants to reap the benefits in the long run. Careful planning and strategy making can maximize your income while haste makes waste.

An inexperienced trader may find it difficult to review stocks especially when it is not aware what it needs to look for. If he does find resources to help him, theory alone cannot help him that much. Practice or practical application is also important to put into action the theory one finds.

PEOPLE TEND **To Become Overconfident**

Binary option gives one the ease of activation, deposit and transfer. Sounds good right? Wrong. This ease of access makes one lenient if not careless.

LEGALITY ISSUES

Some jurisdictions considers online gambling illegal, and they also happen to consider binary options trading as a form of online gambling. So you cannot really trade legally in some states.

TOO MANY CHOICES

Since binary trading caters to local and international assets one can be overwhelmed with the choices. One cannot rely on the general movement of the stock market for it does not reflect individual movements as well. An increase in the stock market is not an assurance that individual stocks will increase as well. 459 words

4

SPOTTING A SCAM

The rule of thumb in binary trading is that when it sounds too good to be true, then it will most likely be a scam.

What is a Scam?

A scam is defined as a dishonest way of obtaining money or anything of value. A fraudulent scheme usually applies confidence tricks and misrepresentations. They often promise a high rate of return bordering on the impossible. This is more common in binary trading.

COMMON BINARY TRADING **Scams**

1. Blocked Trades - Although temporary blockage is not unusual to any brokerage a constant blockage is a sure sign that something is wrong with the company. A brokerage just like any bank operates on the idea that not all its clients will withdraw their money at the same time. However, if this ever happens, the bank and the brokerage should be able to provide enough money to cover all outflows of cash. For banks, their respective central banks assist if the bank is undercapitalized. For brokerage however, there is no such insurance.

If your brokerage is constantly falling short of their payouts to you and your fellow clients it is a sign your broker is undercapitalized and unfortunately it won't be long before your broker goes down with all of your hard-earned money.

2. **Bonus Scams -** Bonuses are not necessarily bad things, and indeed some of them are given. One should really understand the principles behind deposit bonuses. Bonuses supposedly work both ways; the trader would benefit so does the broker. A would be trader is enticed to join the trade with an offer of an incentive. This incentive supposedly increases the trader's capital, giving him a longer string for his portfolio. A bigger capital means an increased trading frequency. This is what makes bonuses work for both trader and broker.

However, this scam makes withdrawing impossible or unrealistic. Sometimes, for the trader to be able to get the bonus he must provide additional capital out of his own pocket.

3. **Account Closure for No Valid Reason**

A broker that changes terms and conditions on a regular basis is a sure sign that something is wrong. One should be wary of a broker that is not regulated.

Having no one to regulate the rules mean the trader's money is at the mercy of the broker. The brokers are creating rules every now and then and before one knows it their hard-earned money may not be returned to them because of unjustified reasons.

4. **Vague regulatory statements**

Some brokerages come up with regulatory statements to make them appear regulated and legal. Some also place their head offices in areas with lax regulations then place some in areas with a solid regulatory body to make it appear as if their operations are legal.

You need to check the statements and if there are questions ask. A company that cannot provide a satisfactory answer to clarification is not a trustworthy company and thus, you should move on to the next broker.

HOW CAN **You Avoid Being Scammed?**

One should practice due diligence before investing their hard-earned money to someone else. In addition to that here are some lists of tips on how to avoid scam artists.

1. Be Realistic

When trying to find a broker to help you with your binary trading needs, look for one that does not offer an early retirement or one that promises money will come into your pockets day in and day out. Trading binary options is not as easy as they make it sound. Binary option is all about fun. Money may come in, but money from this option will not make you a millionaire any time soon. You can make a few thousands a month, but that requires great predictive power, research and analysis of short-term market movements.

· · ·

2. **Stay away from companies that guarantee big profits**

Binary trading is a game of chance. There are two sides to a coin. No one can guarantee profit let alone big ones. Some examples of fraudulent offers are as follows. Read the comment after each example as well:

- **Profit of $2500 a day, every day** – earning depends on your wager. In order for you to earn that high you must bet high as well.
- **A binary market's major benefit is that there is no probability of losses** – wrong. The market, wherever it is located, is unpredictable.
- **If the market moves up or down you will get a profit** - this is possible, but you do need to bet both options at the same time to achieve this.

Do your research

One should find a reputable binary option broker. There are a lot of sites online that provide a list of reliable binary brokers. Check their background, trading history, and feedback from satisfied clients. Wall Street or NYSE might provide you such info as well.

AVOID **companies that have a sketchy history**

They asked you to share your money with them why wouldn't they share their history with you? Make sure you get every detail in written form. Everything should be above board not under.

. . .

LOOKS CAN BE DECEIVING

Most scammers and con artists invest on their looks. A good-looking man or woman is hard to resist right? Beautiful women or gorgeous men explaining they are from Wall Street claiming they trade binary options there are somewhat comforting to a degree. Not. Wall Street traders do not buy binary options, they sell them. Successful traders trade in millions, binary trading ranges within thousands.

NO RISK? **No way**

A firm that promises no risks with their trade is not being honest with their client. Everything is a risk. The goal is not to remove risk, but minimize it.

BE **careful with your transactions**

If anything goes wrong a bank record, a physical address and valid registered credentials is the key to recovering your money just in case. Never transact online when no assurance is given to you to the validity of the business. Bank transfers are safest since opening an account requires a thorough checking of a possible account holder.

5

TEN IMPORTANT STRATEGIES YOU NEED TO KEEP IN MIND TO MAKE SERIOUS MONEY WITH BINARY OPTIONS

The first five chapters of this book covered the basics of binary trading. Preparation is the key to success in this trade. And, of course it wouldn't hurt if one gets a hold of tips and tricks from the masters themselves. Compiled in this chapter would be the top tips and tricks of this trade. Learn it, work it and practice it. However, these are only supplemental. One should practice due diligence when doing some of these tips

1. **Avoid trading binary options when feeling emotional**. This logic applies to almost every endeavor of man. An emotional person is an unreliable person.

2. **Do homework.** Make sure to view the graphs, the charts and all the analyses for a long period. Try to define a pattern if any and learn to interpret the signs. Do all of this BEFORE you begin trading.

. . .

3. **The first sign of a win is all you need.** Once the mark is reached TAKE IT. Do not aim higher or let your stocks linger. You can try doing it some other time.

4. **Listen to what others are saying.** Keep yourself updated and aware of drastic changes in the news. Understand the root cause that way you can corner the market when it rises or falls.

5. **If you are unsure about a trade, do not buy into it.** Gut feeling is not an option when trading. Choose your assets wisely. Although new assets are tempting always choose first the most common. Common assets are most likely discussed in forums more often and through such discussion you can learn a lot. Use this information to your advantage.

6. **Start small and slow.** Do not let a win make you feel indestructible. Employ some sense of self-control. Be grateful with what you earned and do not bite more than you can chew. Avoid long-term binary options until you are ready for it. Choose an hour-long trade or the shorter 60 seconds to maximize profit and minimize risks.

7. **Do not expect to get rich quick.** A make rich quick scheme may prove problematic in the long run. Again, this is a subject of careful reading, analyzing and researching, not sheer luck.

8. **Timing is an important factor in binary trading.** One needs to be able to act fast and should allot

time for trading. Do not leave your short terms open and leave while the iron is hot. Do not invest when the market is volatile or jumpy. A jumpy market can cause great profits, but as the same time great losses too.

9. Know all the strategies. Some of them are briefly described as follows:

- Trading with technical analysis – This strategy uses charts, graphs and the likes. This strategy follows the principle that "the market remembers". This implies that what happens in the past can happen in the present and will happen in the future.

- Trading with trader's tendency indicators- this is normally provided by your broker. This report shows the percentage of traders buying and selling the asset. You need to be careful with this report though for this is not a clear indicator of increase or decrease of the value of an asset. Not because everyone else said so means that it is correct. Try forming your own opinion.

- Trading with fundamental analysis – This strategy focuses on economic statistics as well as the overall economic climate to predict changes in asset values.

- Trading a la martingale. – The martingale is a method of betting wherein the initial investment is increased every time there is a loss until such time that a gain or a win is achieved. This follows the concept of break even. Most experienced trader does not recommend this strategy to beginners and masters alike.

10. Learn how to have fun. It lessens the pressure of earning, makes trading simple and less stressful.

AFTERWORD

I hope this book was able to help you to understand the tricks of binary trading option. As simple as it may sound this type of trading option just like any trading option is risky. Better be prepared than be caught off guard.

The next step is to put into action the list of things mentioned here. To sum it up, remember these steps:

1. Select the asset and the time.
2. Choose your position. You either call (increase) or put (decrease).
3. Choose the amount you want to wager
4. Just wait for the result.

Start slowly and ease your way to the top. Make sure to do your research well. Do not just jump in just because someone said so. When in doubt, you should ask, do your research and study. This book plus your own diligence can make binary trading option your milking cow in no time. Good luck with trading.